FROM PARALYZED TO PROSPEROUS

BY JORGE SIERRA

ISBN: 978-0-578-50155-0

Editors: P31 Publishing, LLC

For more information, please visit www.ajorgesierra.com

Because of the dynamic nature of the internet, any web addresses or links contained in this book may have changed since publication and may no longer be valid.The views expressed in this work are solely those of the author and do not necessarily reflect the views of the publisher, and the publisher disclaims any responsibility for them.

Printed in the United States of America

TABLE OF CONTENTS

CHAPTER 1

❖

Circle of Influence

In early April of 1994, I got picked up on a small posses-
sion charge. I was walking down the street with crack
cocaine in my pocket, and as I was making my way near
courthouse/jail building, I was spotted by some associ-
ates. As I approached them, we were rushed by a couple
of police officers who started asking us, "Where's the gun?
Where's the gun at?" I was confused, because I didn't
know anything about a gun, but come to find out, a few
minutes before I walked up to them, they had been playing with a plastic cap gun, and someone nearby called it
in. We were pushed against the walls, searched, and I got
busted with drugs in my pocket in front of the city court
and jail house. I felt stupid and defeated. I had two years
of selling drugs under my belt with no slip ups, but I got
caught in some mess I had nothing to do with anyway. It
wasn't until after my processing that I heard the metal cell
door close and realized the depth of my crimes. I started to understand that I could really end up doing federal
time. After a few minutes, I pulled myself together and

made some phone calls to see if anyone could bail me out, and by the grace of God, my grandmother was able to come down and get me out of jail.

A month later, on the first of May, I woke up, still half asleep and trying to figure out what was going on. My head was pounding, and after a few minutes I realized why I was so disoriented. Some of my gang member friends and I threw a party last night. On top of the party being a success and having a good time, nothing crazy happened despite getting into an argument with some rival gang members a week prior who *knew* about the party. I felt like I was on top of the world because even though several people told me they heard about some retaliation plots, and I had dreams about what was going to happen at the party, nothing happened. Plus, even if it did, I was surrounded by a group of people who were down to go through whatever, whenever, so it would be whatever if we got approached at the party. A few seconds later, I whispered to myself, "DANG! I got court tomorrow morning!" I then told myself I needed to call my mother to see if she could go with me to my court appearance that next day even though I didn't want to call her. Because I was a minor, I needed her there.

I made my way outside to smoke a cigarette after cleaning up in the bathroom, and while out there, I overheard two women talking about how God forgives. I gave a quick thought to everything I'd done in life, jumped into their conversation and said, "God would never forgive me. I've done way too much. I promise you that." They turned, and one of them said, "Nah, you're wrong. As long as you repent, and you're genuinely sorry in your heart for everything you've done... He'll forgive you. I promise *you* that." I shook my head, and I told them, "Nah, trust me. I'm too far gone." After that, our conversation ended, it was about noon, and I told myself I had to actually get my day started beginning with that phone call to my mother.

I can still hear the conversation I had with myself *just* before I got shot. Right before I heard my mother screaming, and the sheriffs grabbed me and everyone involved. I remember asking myself, *"You see how he's looking at you? I don't care, man. I promise you. I don't care, man. I'm about to set it off if they keep looking at me like I'm crazy. I'm not the one! You see those four guys who just walked through the set of doors?!"* All four of them were from the Sólidos gang, my rivals as a member of the Latin Kings gang in Connecticut. For the last several years we had been at war, and it had been *bloody*. For the last couple of months, I had people coming up to me telling me I should watch my back and to be careful because the word on the street was that there was a price on my head. As the sheriff started dragging us down the stairs at the Bristol Courthouse, I was saying to myself, *"It's about to get real,"* and once I got halfway down the staircase, I got a really bad feeling in my stomach that everything was about to get *insane*. I kept telling myself that the situation was about to get real, and once I saw the set of doors at the bottom of the staircase, I knew things were definitely about to go south. There was no turning back now. *What was I supposed to do? Should I tell the sheriffs I didn't want to go outside? How would I look if I didn't fight? Like a coward. I couldn't go out like that. I could never come back from it no matter how many more crimes I committed to prove how tough and committed I was.*

Once I got to the other side of those double doors, I heard my mother scream, "Gun! Gun! Gun!" Naturally, I dove in front of my mother to protect her and that's when the first bullet pierced my body causing everything around me to go silent. Shortly after, the second bullet tore into my body and stopped me in my tracks. The only thing I could hear was my own voice in saying, *"Jorge you need to run! They're going to kill you!"*

I tried to run, but my knees got weak, my torso got loose, and I collapsed at my mother's feet. As I lay sprawled out on the ground, several more bullets pierced my back, and blood poured out of me like an unattended faucet. As I laid there gasping for air, I asked myself how did I end up in this situation. I thought back a few months prior when I was living the fast life, and women, money, and drugs were all I cared about. I felt unstoppable as if I had an *S* on my chest like Superman. Every crime I committed had a consequence. A lot of lives, especially the ones that were intertwined with mine, were changed due to me being surrounded by pure evil and destruction.

I hadn't lived with my mother since I was three years old, and she dropped me off to live with my grandmother. We were much less a mother-son duo and more of a brother-sister one, but she still felt so much fear and pain that she urinated on herself when I fell to her feet. My life changed instantly. I was no longer worrying about people's opinions of me. It did not matter whether I looked like a punk or was viewed as a snitch. I no longer cared about the opinions of the dudes who got me here. All I was thinking was that I was going to die, and that I couldn't feel my legs.

I realized I finally found the circle of influence that was going to educate me on how to live a life of value. I wanted nothing more than to be surrounded with positive energy and to learn how to take myself to another level. To sit in a room full of like-minded individuals whose only agenda was to live the triple double life was a blessing. Life is what you make of it. Your decisions now will affect your life tomorrow. If you are in a situation that you know is not healthy or empowering, it is time to reevaluate your direction and take action. Look around you right now and ask yourself a few questions: *Who am I? What do I stand for? Do I create value in others' space including my own? Who is in my circle of influence?* If you answer any of these questions with the facts of a negative lifestyle, do not allow yourself to wait until it is too late. Create a plan of action that will allow you to surround yourself with the right circle of influence. It is time to take control of your own life and start winning because when you allow other people's negative opinions to dictate your life, you will lose every time. As individuals, we have the ability to make decisions and choose the kind of days and life we want to have, and too often, we sabotage our own lives. We get very comfortable with making the decision to live with a negative mindset. You *have* to learn to control your own life because making decisions based on someone else's approval can cloud your judgement, and you can lose the opportunity to receive a blessing. Imagine losing out on a great opportunity because you couldn't take two seconds to collect yourself before making your next move or saying your next words.

CHAPTER 2

✧

Your Decisions Design Your Destiny

One of the most valuable lessons I learned set in the moment I opened my eyes in the hospital room and realized how my previous decisions led me here. There were machines connected to my body and a breathing tube taped to my face. I couldn't move, but with every breath, my body felt as if it was collapsing in on me. I started to panic, I frantically searched the room, and my blood pressure started to increase. The nurse came in and tried to calm me down by reassuring me everything was going to be fine, but I couldn't stop wondering if I was dying. The more I panicked caused more people in the room to cry, and it became harder to breathe and calm down. All I could do was replay all the decisions that got me here. I went from a football huddle in high school to a gang huddle on the block.

Before I started running the streets, I was a starting defensive tackle on the freshman high school football team for the

Bristol Central Rams. The practices were long, and our coach was tough, but I loved every minute of being on the team. No matter what the score was, or how practice went, he'd always remind us that our talents would take us places, but our character would keep us there. Crazily enough, it made sense on both sides of the life I had lived so far. My ability to do crime got me into a gang, and the person I'd become after I got in the gang kept me there.

At home, education was not something we celebrated or even discussed, so, when my grades dropped, and I was informed that I could not play any sports at school until I was at the proper academic level, I decided school wasn't for me anymore. Instead of just taking ownership of my situation and making the proper adjustments, I "copped out" with a sad excuse and decided to quit. This was just the first of *many* decisions that led me down the path to getting gunned down at the age of seventeen. Even though school was not something I particularly liked, I regret not completing high school. I chose the streets over my family, education, and everything else in my life. As a young teen, I struggled with making the right decisions in life because it seemed like everyone around me glorified the street life, and it was so much easier to blend in with the crowd instead of trying to stand out and create my own destiny.

Deep inside, I *always* wanted to do the right thing and be successful at everything I tried, but it was always a challenge because I didn't know what success *looked* like. All I knew was my environment. Growing up in poverty without a father and being raised by my grandmother, I developed this mindset that was justification for my actions, and once I did, no one could change that. I decided to surround myself with individuals who had no goals, dreams, or core values in life. They valued hanging out, getting high, and wasting their lives. It was so easy to blame everyone for my situation. However, I *always* knew that I was responsible for the decisions I made not just after waking up in the hospital.

I can still remember the shock and horror that I felt at the moment that the doctor told me that I would never walk again. I remember that moment as if it was yesterday. From the look in the doctor's eyes, I knew that he was not about to give me good news as he closed the door quietly and walked towards my hospital bed. "Jorge, there is no easy way to tell you this. You've been paralyzed." Once the word, "paralyzed," left his mouth, the room became silent, my stomach fell to the floor, and I felt as if I was going to throw it back up. I didn't know any paraplegics, and I struggled mightily to accept that life as I knew it would never be the same. Deep inside my heart, I knew this was my new reality. I didn't consider how the consequences of living a street life would affect not only me, but also my loved ones, and as if waking up a seventeen-year-old paraplegic was not life changing enough, I found out that I was going to be a father. From that moment forward, I knew I had to make changes in my life, which is how I ended up in barber school a little while later.

I was rolling by the barber school and saw a beautiful woman dressed in all white outside the shop. In an effort to be cute, I decided to tell her I needed a nurse because I thought she was one. She looked at me like she was going to call the cops if I didn't back off, so I relaxed my body language a bit, and then she told me that she wasn't a nurse, but she was in school to be a barber. I told my friend to help me out of the car, so I could take a walk inside and once I got inside, all of the things that attracted me to barbering started to come to mind. I was intrigued by the flexibility of hours, the charisma of the barbers, and the super relaxed and comfortable dress code in the shop. I didn't really have intentions of signing up for barbering school. It was a big joke honestly, but when the receptionist called for the instructor to come to the front, that's when things got a little more tangible for me.

She had me follow her to the clinic floor, showed me around, and introduced me to a few of her current students. At the end of the tour, she asked me if I was going to sign up for school, and I looked at her like she was absolutely crazy, and she simply told me, "Life is what you make it." After a few seconds, I finally said, "I'm interested, I just don't know what that looks like," and the concern that I had was clearly because I was a paraplegic. I didn't think it was a logical career path for me. Seeing my doubts, she walked to the back and came back out with an office chair, two pillows, two phone books, and duct tape. She taped the pillows and books together, stacked them on top of the office chair, and taped all of that together to create a custom chair for me. She then looked at me and asked, "Can you move from your wheelchair to this chair?" I had core strength, so I was able to move myself, and once I got up onto the chair, she pushed me close to the barber chair and asked me how it felt. I said "It feels good." Then she told me, "You know, you don't have to walk around the barber chair. It adjusts in height and reclines to fit you as the barber. If you really want to be a barber, I'm here to make you a barber."

Because of my past decisions and friends, adjusting to school was difficult. As school started, I had outside things affecting my schooling, and I couldn't afford school monetarily or when it came to the outcome of my life and the life of my daughter. I came to the realization that I needed to cut off certain friends and take my new career path seriously. I had a lot of work to do, I had to learn how to communicate with people and how to not only cut hair, which is a task in itself, but also I had to learn to do it sitting down, which was a challenge unique to me in my new setting.

I really had to take a look at who I was and assess everything that was going on around me. The one thing I knew for certain was that I wanted to give my daughter the best life I could provide whether or not I was in a wheelchair. Self-assessing became a really big factor in my life from that point forward. I learned that life is going to hit you! The question you should ask yourself when it does is, "When and how am I going to react?" If you cannot answer the following questions, you have to truly self-assess your character:

1) *Are you who you say you are?*

2) *What are your core values?*

3) *What are your dreams*

4) *Who depends on you?*

5) *What is your gift?*

Even though I knew I wanted to change, I would discover soon it was going to take everything in me, and it most certainly was not going to happen overnight. Change will not happen overnight. Trust the process and always have a vision in mind.

Even outside of your physical actions and words, you have to be careful of the decisions you make. Social media has become a big issue in today's world and it's because a lot of people don't understand that just like your words and actions, you can't take back what's put out into the cyberverse. Politicians, teachers, business owners, models, pageant winners, and professional athletes have all been stripped of their positions, respect, and accolades for things they've tweeted, or sent out in the past that they thought would either never see the light of day or be forgotten about. Before you act on impulse and send that nude photo, sexually explicit text, racist comment, or plain hateful tweet, Facebook post, comment or personal message, understand the depth of your decision and the fact that you will never get to take that back. Even if you are allowed to delete it, who's to say that it hasn't been screenshotted, shared, or saved just to be pulled out when you're on top of the world? That comment, that post, or that picture no longer belongs to you when you press send. Control what you can control! YOUR DECISIONS DESIGN YOUR DESTINY!

CHAPTER 3

❖

Self Control

Self Control, noun: the ability to control oneself, in particular one's emotions and desires or the expression of them in one's behavior, especially in difficult situations

I remember in middle school there were two brothers, Jose and Pedro. Both of them were in one of my classes, and for whatever reason, they would always feel the need to bully me. They would call me names in Spanish so no one else, especially the teacher, would understand. They would try to trip me, throw my stuff from the desk to the floor, and at times, physically shove me around and into things. I was so miserable during that class period. I never told the teacher on them because I didn't want to get in trouble even though I was not the one instigating the situation. I didn't want to fight or have a sit down with the teachers about it. I just wanted to be left alone. Instead of getting an adult involved, I let the anger build up, and I reacted by fighting Jose and Pedro one day. I never spoke up, and I never let anyone know that I was being bullied for months, and because I didn't, the day I defended myself, it all seemed as If I was the one with the problem. The only thing the teacher saw was me hitting Jose and Pedro. I got sent to the office for hitting students. Once I arrived in the principal's office, I tried to plead my case, but I was viewed as a liar. You see, the only thing that the teacher saw was me retaliating by hitting Jose and Pedro; she did not see them pushing me. In her eyes, she saw me hit them first, and I got suspended while José and Pedro were left with no punishment. I was angry that after I was bullied for weeks and months, the one time that I actually defended myself I got in trouble.

Once I saw the Sólidos at the courthouse, I could not take control of my pride and ego, and that is the *only* reason I was shot outside the courthouse that day. I looked at them as they were throwing gang signs at me while my mother stood next to me in the courtroom, and that's how the altercation began that led to me being shot. I want you to pause and think about this scenario for one moment. I was not being *physically* hurt, but I was being disrespected by *words* and *hand gestures*. My pride and ego were *bruised*, and I acted in my emotions, and we know that's a recipe for failure. Right before I was gunned down in front of my mother, I had multiple opportunities to change the outcome, but I *never* chose a different path. I let my emotions get the best of me even when my life was being threatened. I didn't have any control over myself or anything else.

My pride and ego were the main reasons I got gunned down. You see, that day was bound to happen one way or another because that was the path I had set for myself. It is a known fact that living a life full of drug use, drug dealing, gun toting, and gang involvement can only lead to three negative outcomes:

1. Being behind bars for life
2. Being six feet under
3. Being in a wheelchair

The problem with a lot of us is that our pride, ego, and emotions take over our minds, and we no longer think logically. When you act on those things instead of taking the time to think and make the right choice, you lose big time. Once you fill yourself with pride and a huge ego, you stop creating value, and instead, you create a version of yourself that's disrespectful, hurtful, and abusive to those around you. You stop walking in your purpose.

Now, when you are facing any situation, ask yourself a series of questions:

1. Do I have a valid reason to get angry or am I in my emotions?
2. Am I going to regret my actions?
3. Am I creating value in anyone's life, including my own life?

4. Am I giving anyone or anything the power to throw me off track?

5. Am I doing everything it takes to be the best version of myself?

The first day back home from the hospital after getting shot was very exciting, but the fun quickly came to an end. As I sat in the living room entertaining family, my wheelchair tilted back, and I fell to the floor. It did not physically hurt, but my pride and ego were bruised. It became hard to avoid letting my emotions get the best of me. I realized that I had to start being conscious of acting in ways, saying, or doing things that I would regret afterwards.

When we get upset, our mind raises the red flags, and we start to want to scream, yell, and fight. Even if we know as plain as day that we're in the wrong and should apologize, our pride and ego can keep us from apologizing. Stop thinking situations are always about you. Just know that sometimes your pride and ego will get hurt, but if that is all that gets hurt, you are truly winning in life. Once you realize that it is not about you, but it is about how you serve others, you will stop feeling used by others. You will stop giving others the power to dictate how you feel. You are the only one who holds the power to control your thoughts, which indeed controls your emotions. Keep away from individuals who are being disrespectful, manipulative, or negative. If you work on making more decisions with fewer emotions and strictly facts, you will see growth in all aspects of your life.

When you work on yourself and invest into personal, professional, or business development, you will feed your higher consciousness, and your pride and ego will be replaced with the correct energy. You will begin to ask yourself:

1. Where do my thoughts and emotions originate?

2. Are my emotions getting in the way of my growth in life?

3. What are my core values and are they aligned with my pride and ego?

The first two weeks living at my grandmother's house after my incident were unpleasant for everyone. Getting adjusted to life as a paraplegic would be challenging for anyone, not just me. Being a new paraplegic back in my grandmother's house and living there with so many people had me emotionally drained and unbalanced. The mood was always tense at the house. I always concentrated on avoiding arguments with anyone because I knew it would cost me the roof over my head. However, my pride and ego would not let me ignore any comments that I felt were disrespectful towards me. Many times, I would get into disagreements with everyone including my grandmother, which led to me getting kicked out of the house for a few months.

Your emotions will never allow you to see the clear truth in any situation. Taking control of how someone or something makes you feel is life changing. Once you can control your emotions, you will have total control of your life's journey. My pride and arrogance caused me to be a homeless, seventeen-year-old, paraplegic new father. My pride and ego caused me to move constantly because I believed that everyone else had a problem except me. Oftentimes, I slept on the floor. At times, I would make believe I was sleeping on the sofa just to make myself feel more comfortable. After some time, all my family moved to Massachusetts, and I was left alone in Connecticut with just my pride. That loneliness eventually caused me to have a bad attitude and negative outlook on life.

It is so easy to put the blame on others while not taking responsibility for your own actions, but once you make a decision in your mind, and you act on it, you *have* to face the consequences no matter what problems occur. The one person who you have when you're going through all of this is you, and you are the one person you have to learn to count on. You cannot give up on yourself based on whether or not someone is there for you. Roaming Connecticut for a couple years made my health situation worse. As a paraplegic, you become accustomed to chronic urinary tract infections, which lead to frequent hospital stays. My health complications got worse, so I was in need of stability in my life. I needed to leave the street life, and I needed to stop smoking weed and being lazy so I could change my life and try to correct my mistakes to the best of my power. At this point, the wear and tear I caused to my body was finally catching up to me.

Once I made the decision to follow my grandmother to Massachusetts, things started to look promising. All I needed to do was to control my temper and be productive. A few months passed while I was living in Massachusetts. Everything was going well until I had one or two disagreements with my grandmother and got kicked out of the house. The difference this time around was that I was in a totally new state, and I didn't know anyone. Once again, I allowed my emotions to get the best of me. Due to issues at the house, my grandmother decided to pack her stuff and leave for the Bronx, NY. My pride and ego still did not allow me to see how bad my behavior was towards people. The ultimate challenge in life is to learn from mistakes and avoid making them again. To promote positive changes in yourself, ask the following questions:

1. What are some characteristics I would like to change about myself?

2. Name 3 people who would benefit from me changing my behaviors?

3. Do I love myself? If not, what are some things that can lead me to love myself?

To this very day, as a business owner, husband, father, community leader and man of God, I have to be very aware of the situations and people with whom I surround myself, and it's a constant choice of self control. I could easily disregard my status as a married man and surround myself with single women and fall to temptation, but I instilled in my mind enough self-control to know that I don't need to be in that environment, and I avoid it. I know that I have a daughter, and I want her to grow up knowing what true love and respect are from a man to a woman. I'm going to be her first example, and I set that example with my wife. I could let myself fall back into my ways of smoking weed and getting drunk for fun, but as a pillar in my community, that would look terrible, and it could send the complete wrong message to some other young man or woman looking up to me and land them in the exact same position I worked so hard to leave. The bottom line is it's always easy to let someone else take control and just go with the flow of whatever, but the consequence will always be there in the end for the part you played in the mess they may or may not create of your life.

CHAPTER 4

❖

The Fear Factor

My grandmother was a five foot, five inch New York native, and she did *not* like to repeat herself. I can remember when I was about six years old, I would be outside playing, and I'd hear my grandmother call for me to come inside. Usually, she wanted me to wash the dishes or take a shower, and I didn't like doing either, which is why eventually I started playing deaf. "Jorge! Jorge!" she would yell, but if she called me three times and I didn't answer, I *knew* that I would be in some serious trouble. I remember one time she called me to go to the basement and check on my uncle and grandfather, but I was so afraid of the pitch black darkness down there that I stood at the top of the basement stairs just looking into it. My fear would not let me move, but the fear of the consequences if I didn't do what she asked were much heavier, so I went down there and I checked on them like she asked. That was the first time I remember feeling fear inside my soul and the first time I got over it.

The majority of the time fear isn't even real. It is just an emotion that can be controlled. For example, it was scary for

me when I moved to a new state in which I didn't know anyone, didn't have any income, and didn't have a home. I was
also a first-time father who had no education, and on top of all
that, I was paralyzed. I was terrified, but in my heart I knew I
had two choices. Either I had to succumb to my circumstances
and allow my situation to define me as a person, or I had to
follow my ambition to be someone who actually could create
value in others, especially in my daughter and me. I had become so tired of making excuses, and I decided to give this
next phase in my life everything I had for a chance at a better
life. The fear of change completely went away when I decided
that life is truly what you make of it.

The first step I took was to go get my GED. Once I started classes, I started to meet different kinds of people than my
normal circle of friends. It felt nice to be around those types
of people who were like-minded when it came to being successful. Even after a few months, while I was still struggling
to get a stable place to live, and I had no money, I didn't let
any of that put fear in my spirit. I kept telling myself that if
I kept showing up, things would get better. One day, a lady
showed up to the GED program to recruit people to work at
an agency that advocates for physically challenged individuals
like me, and after speaking with her, she was very impressed
with my interview and decided to give me an opportunity to
work. If I hadn't tried something different by enrolling in the

GED program, I wouldn't have met other like-minded people interested in bettering their lives.

My biggest fear over the first half of my paraplegic life was my physical appearance because I was afraid that people would dislike me or be afraid of me because of my paraplegic status. I was afraid that I wouldn't be able to do all of the things that I needed to do to help me recover as much as possible from being injured. I felt like I would be looked at differently if I went to physical therapy and had to do some of those exercises. With any spinal cord injury, the doctors tell you that you have to do as much physical movement as possible without overdoing it and hurting yourself within the first three years so that you sustain the injury because if you're going to get anything back that you lost from the injury, you're going to get it back in that time frame. However, my mental wheelchair was so strong that I didn't move from that chair in twenty-five years. The day I decided to face my fears and stop being afraid of all the 'What ifs?,' I was able to walk, I was able to stand, and I was able to do it all just by changing the way I thought about myself.

Sometimes, you just need to look with a different perspective. Now, things were starting to look brighter. I knew it was going to be a long process, but it felt amazing to start carving out a plan for the rest of my life. The right Information always changes situations. Conquering my fears gave me options. Now, I was not only educating myself, but also I had an actual job that could pay for my new apartment. After just one year of exposing myself to the right environment, I was able to start planning on raising my daughter. Consider the following questions when you evaluate the impact of fear on your life:

1. What is your biggest fear?
2. For how long have you been paralyzed in making decisions?
3. What are the steps you need to start so you can "level up"?
4. Are you ready to make an impact?
5. What are the reasons fear can no longer be a factor in your decision making?

Remember, the majority of the time fear is not real. We get scared with assumptions of the difficulty of the struggles that we will experience in our life, so we do not act. Life is full of wins and losses; it is how the world turns. Winning is not the only form of success. Losing is part of success as well. As they say, *I never lose, I just learn.* Your only fear in life should be the fear of not trying. Do not be a *coulda/shoulda* type of individual! It is very important to always look at your options. Not trying is never an option!

Fear comes in so many different forms, but my biggest fear is letting a situation get the best of me and not trying to make it better. I am accustomed to losing in life, but that was never an excuse for me to stop trying to make things better. I am physically paralyzed and cannot move, but the majority of average people allow their fears to paralyze them in ways that they stay stuck mentally.

Not allowing yourself to be paralyzed by fear will always give you the ability to move and create value for a better life. Insecurity and self-doubt caused me to feel disabled, and I do not just mean in the physical form.

CHAPTER 5

❖

Self Love (Take a Stand Against Bullies)

In the last couple of chapters, I shared some personal experiences that changed my life for better or worse. Looking back on those experiences, I realize that one thing they taught me was that it does not matter how insane your situation is at the moment, you *always* have an option. It may not be the option you want at the moment, but the better option is always there and eventually helps to create better opportunities for your future.

My grandmother would move from town to town when I was young, and it was very challenging for me to make friends at every new school I attended. It seemed as if every time I got comfortable in any neighborhood or school, it would be time to move, and I would have to start all over again. My routine consisted of meeting new people in the neighborhoods, new teachers, and new classmates. Eventually, it started to feel like a never ending déjà vu.

Because I was always the new kid in school, it was challenging for me to make friends. The more I moved, the less confidence I had in interacting with others. I would find myself in situations with individuals bullying me or trying to bully me simply because my skin was different from everybody else. I would attend schools that were either 80% Caucasian or 80% African-American, and being Hispanic made it challenging for me across the board. Not only did I have problems speaking proper English, but my complexion was always too many shades darker or lighter than that of my peers. After school, my home life wasn't all that glamorous either. There was constant chaos, arguing, fist-fighting. and drugs, and I didn't feel like that's where I belonged either.

I woke up feeling out of place and walked through school feeling the same way. That constant rejection always made me feel like there was a problem with me. I felt like I wasn't as valuable as others or that my life didn't didn't matter as much as everyone else's life. All I ever wanted was to be accepted at home and in school. I always thought to myself, *Why do I have to be so different from everyone else?*

As an adult, I realized that being different is a beautiful thing. People tend to feel threatened when they encounter someone or something different from what they are accustomed to experiencing. Being different is the key to walking in our purpose. If we all looked and acted the same and had the same gifts, what would be the purpose of anything?

Bullies tend to be very insecure and haven't the slightest idea how special they truly are. They are usually going through the same kind of pain they're causing you. Whether it was by another school peer or someone in their home, they've been hurt physically, verbally, emotionally, or all the above, and because they stop being comfortable with who they are, they tend to bully others to make themselves feel better.

No one has the right to verbally or physically assault you in anyway. You have the obligation to stand up for yourself by addressing the problem right at the moment and letting someone know what happened. Regardless of whom you tell, tell someone! If you are being mistreated in any particular way, and you are not comfortable, you have to speak up. More importantly, what I learned is to embrace differences; we are all unique in our own way. People will judge you and treat you a certain way when they do not understand you. It is up to you to decide how you respond to it. Once you learn how to love yourself fully and completely embrace who you are, everything else will come together full circle. The opinions of others will not bother you when you value yourself.

By the time I got to high school, I was so focused on being invisible that the only thing that caught my attention was the football team. I didn't want to be laughed at because of my clothes, shoes, and hair cut, so I walked quickly with my head down during class changes. When I wasn't ducking eyes in the hallways or hiding my haircut in my hood, I was paying attention to football staff and players and listening for their announcements. I enjoyed watching and playing football, so I tried out and made the football team freshman year. I played for the entire season, and we had an amazing record that year with one loss, one tie game, and victories in the rest of the games. My plan was to involve myself with many sports so I could just keep myself busy and entertained while I went to high school. After football, I wanted to join the wrestling team, but I wasn't eligible because I didn't have the grades I needed to play high school sports. I had no real interest in school after that, so I decided to drop out. The only amazing time I actually had was the time spent on the football field. Once I walked out, I never came back again. At the time, I felt like I was the man. Dropping out gave me a sense of freedom. I really did not understand how badly I was jeopardizing my entire future by not finishing high school. Like many of us, I let my situation define who I was at the time. I let the problems at home and the problems in school determine how I reacted.

As you continue reading this book, I want you to question yourself on how important your life *really* is to you. You might say to yourself: *I am depressed. I dislike myself. I do not have a reason to live. No one loves me. Why should I stick around? Why should I go through the process?* The reason why is that your perspective needs to change. Even though you experience storms, pain, and adversity in life, you have the power to determine how you live your life. You determine whether you are going to be sad or happy. You have the choice to give yourself a better quality of life. You cannot continue blaming everybody for not living your best life. Even if others are at fault, you have to take ownership and create a better space for yourself. You may have been bullied, or you may have been a bully. You may look or sound different from others, or you may come from a background of poverty, but you control your own destiny. You have everything inside of you to be successful in life. Stop letting anyone or anything get you out of character because it will continue to cause you to lose in life.

You have the power to work on yourself daily and become a better version of yourself. That is how you WALK into greatness. I am here to share with you that if you are true to who you are and have goals, dreams, and aspirations of greatness, you can achieve anything in life. All you need is to go through the process even if, at times, the process becomes painful. The pain stretches you to a point where you will see growth. Anything worth having comes with a price. People are going to disappoint you, and things are not going to go your way at times, but remember, any excuse you give yourself does not excuse you from being great and walking in your purpose while you create a legacy. Living in one of the best countries in the world, you see individuals come from nothing and make it all the way to the top. The resources are all around you, and that gives you the same opportunities as anyone else to become who you want to be in life. You have the same 24 hours as everyone else, and you breathe and bleed the same as everyone else. The only thing stopping you from being who you want to become in life is you and only you. How is that possible? Well, you have not made the decision to be who you want to become yet. You are still blaming everyone else for your situation. You may be saying: *My father or my mother is not in my life. My family did not have the proper finances to live an average life. Someone has physically or mentally abused me. I am not accepted because I look different.* However, you cannot allow those thoughts to stop you from achieving your goals.

It is important to know the importance of your circle of influence, character, pride, ego, and fear in your development so that you can realize the purpose of living a phenomenal lifestyle. We get accustomed to complaining about our situation but not acting on solutions. We complain about not having money, but we are not willing to go work. We complain because we do not have a good paying job, but we do not expose ourselves to environments that will equip and empower us to level up. I remember in my early 20's, I had friends who always looked at life as if it was not fair. We used to sit around smoking weed and talking about how cool it would be to have money. We would talk for hours about how awesome it would be to have cars and houses and be able to travel around the world. We never talked about how we could make those things actually happen in our lives. As time passed, I looked around and realized I was not going to make any changes in my life unless

I changed my behaviors. I realized I had to change my whole outlook in life if I was going to have any positive outcomes.

The first step to becoming the best version of yourself is to work from the inside out. You may be the victim in multiple areas of life, but it's not impossible to become a victor. Life can seem incredibly unfair to some people who are dealing with challenges at home and in school, but it is important to remember who you are. Do not allow the negative words of other people to distract you from your destiny. Like me, you may move a lot from school to school and have problems making friends. Your home life may not be ideal, and you may feel that school is the safest place for you to be yourself. Maybe, you get teased by a bully at school who does not respect the fact that you are wonderful and unique. You were created with a purpose, and you can overcome those situations by staying focused on your goals, remembering your greatness, and aligning yourself with positive people who will support you and care for you.

My next step was my physical appearance. The gym was the perfect place to see how people benefited by loving themselves. In the gym, I see all types of individuals with different goals. Some want to trim their bodies and some want to bulk up or maintain what they have, but whatever their goal is, they are there at the gym to achieve that goal. Since I am in a wheelchair, I get a lot of folks staring at me while I work out in the gym. At first, I was very uncomfortable with people staring at me because not only was I in a wheelchair, but also I was uncomfortable with how I looked. After I finally started to see results, the looks didn't really bother me because I felt better about how I looked, but it all started with me loving myself enough to take that first step to work on my self-confidence.

CHAPTER 6

❖

Tired of Being Tired

Growing up, my uncle and grandfather would sit on the porch, drink, and share stories of how someone they knew made it big time. They always told stories of the homeboys with whom they hung out as kids who ended up in jail, dead, or were confined to a wheelchair. I would sit and watch as these two grown men admired other grown men who lived lifestyles of murder, hate, drugs, and violence. I know at times it is really hard to do anything that you have not seen or done in your life already. It is so easy to mimic everything we see around us. Is that unique? We all have a different perspective when it comes to how winning looks. I need you to imagine your wildest dreams. Plan your life from beginning to end. How will your home look? Envision the smallest to the biggest details. Think of the color, size, and location of the house. When you get specific with your goals, you get specific with your footsteps, and it gets harder to let anything or anyone throw you off.

The reality is life is what you make it. You can sit in your misery, or you can decide to take action! You can give your life to drugs, gang, guns, money, violence, and sex, or you can go against all the negativity by investing into yourself. I heard a gentleman speaking to a group of people telling them that he is thankful for the decisions he made as a 30-year-old. He said he made those decisions and sacrifices so that his 40-year-old self could benefit from them.

The reason you are not winning and most likely will continue to lose for years to come is that you are more concerned with parties, mall trips, movies, and any other distractions that come to your mind. Fun comes first to many, but that is why they go through life being average always wondering why they do not win in life. You cannot want different results but continue with the same behaviors.

Do not become comfortable with having an average mindset and living an average life. You are phenomenal and meant to make a phenomenal impact in life. You are amazing and are truly a king or queen in your space. Always think about royalty living. Work on being a better version of yourself than yesterday's version. The moment you are truly tired of being tired is when you will sacrifice who you are to become who you want to be. It is your life. Take control of it and create your own reality. Ask yourself the following questions as you strive to become better:

1. What are 3 different behaviors I have to change to WALK in my purpose?

2. What are 3 things I am tired of in my life?

3. What are 3 things I can control and do to make my present situation better?

One winter, during a state of emergency, I was headed to one of many couches I was crashing on at the time because I was homeless, and the snow from the blizzard was so heavy that I couldn't even see five feet in front of me. There was just a thick white shield of snow on all sides of me. The wind was howling, and I didn't have any gloves or blizzard-proof clothes. As I made my way down the sidewalk, I got stuck in the snow. I couldn't move forward or backwards. My hands were frozen, and my face was frozen, I was cold all over, and I just broke down right there on the sidewalk. My tears were the only warmth I was getting, and I felt so defeated. A few minutes later, a car appeared out of nowhere, and a man came up to me concerned for my safety. He asked if I needed help getting where I was going, but I was so angry that I told him, 'Nah, I'm good. I don't want your help." He insisted on helping me. He said, "I'm not just gonna leave you on the sidewalk, this blizzard is crazy. Let me help you," However, I insisted on staying stuck and cold. He finally said to me, "I *can't* leave you here knowing you're stuck and can't move. At least, let me help you get onto the street. It's been plowed so you can actually rolls your wheels and get yourself where you're going for the night." I finally agreed, and he helped me out of the snow and onto the street. Then, he continued home, and I haven't seen him since.

That became the breaking point for me. I was tired of everything. I was tired of being tired, I was tired of being broke, I was tired of being paraplegic and wheeling myself across the city up and down hills and in all kinds of weather, and I was the most tired of not being able to depend on anyone. I was pushing my wheelchair through an empty city street in the middle of the blizzard that shut it down. I was blinded from understanding how heavy the snow was with blue skin, and I was two seconds from being frostbitten. All I could think was that this would be the last time that I would get stuck like this. I decided that I was going to work for my own car and house, and I would never be without either again. Ever.

At times, going through life can feel as if you are getting a beat down from multiple people at the same time. It can feel as if you are going through a fight that just will not end. You feel the punches, elbows, and kicks coming your way,and at times, they catch you by surprise. I know what it's like to be tired of being tired. You are tired of looking around and not having someone or something to call your own, and you are tired of life just not being fair. Below are five steps for breaking this cycle and becoming phenomenal:

1. Get tired of being tired.

2. Self-assess.

3. Find your reason to want more (WHY).

4. Get comfortable with being uncomfortable.

5. Establish consistency in your routine.

CHAPTER 7

❖

Not Living Life With Regret

For as long as I can remember, my grandmother always made sure there was food on the table when it was time to eat. We didn't have much, but the little we had was because grandmother made it happen. Around the end of the month, things would get tight at home with food and bills, so oftentimes, she would sit in the living room with the phone in one ear delegating tasks to everyone else in the house, and by the time we were done, Chinese food was on the dinner table. Watching her taught me at an early age that nobody is going to come to your front door and hand you success.

In my eyes, she was unstoppable, so when I received the call that she had passed away at the ripe young age of 55 from a massive heart attack, I was devastated. My grandmother and I hadn't spoken since she left from Massachusetts to live in New York, and the week before receiving the call of her passing, she called me and left me a message saying, "Listen, punk, I am still your grandmother, so call me." It had been more than a year since we spoke, and when I heard the message, I smiled because I loved hearing her voice. I said to myself, *I'll call her back*. Unfortunately, I forgot, and a week later, she passed. One of my sisters called me and told me she had some news for me, and immediately, I felt the pressure in my chest because I just knew it wasn't good. I was devastated. I cried, punched, and kicked, because she was really gone, and I never got a chance to tell the woman who raised me how much she meant to me. Life taught me a valuable lesson that day: Your loved ones are not here forever so stop being so angry and tell them that you love them.

Since that day, I view life differently. I realized that time on this Earth is limited, and while you are here, it's your duty to create value for yourself and for those you love. I know you may be going through it, and I know there are things inside of you that may need healing. If you do not handle the problem, it will be very difficult to achieve success with your family, mind, body, and soul. When you are stuck in pain, it will slowly destroy you if you do not let go. Control the things you can. It is time you take what belongs to you. Having nothing to lose and everything to gain gives you leverage. My grandma always told me not to let anyone dictate my life. She taught me to think for myself and to be a leader, not a follower. Since I was a child, it was clear to me that in life you have to create your own opportunities.

It is time you take yourself to the highest level you can attain. It is time to say to yourself: *Who am I? What do I stand for? Who do I want to become?* It really does not matter where you begin. You always have a chance to achieve greatness as long as you have air in your lungs.

CHAPTER 8

❖

Get Comfortable with Being Uncomfortable

In my opinion, the only way to bring yourself to a higher level is to get comfortable with being uncomfortable, and I had to learn that at seventeen. During the first week of being in the hospital after getting gunned down as the doctors and nurses told me about the many adjustments I was going to have to make, the only thing I could think about was how hard my life was about to get as a paraplegic. As the nurse explained how and why I had to use catheters for the rest of my life, all I could do was cry. If you are not familiar with what a catheter is, it is a 16-inch plastic or rubber tube that paraplegics insert into their private areas and into their bodies all the way to their bladder in order to urinate. Without the device, a paraplegic cannot urinate. Using a catheter is a very involved process which requires a lot of patience, skill, and careful hygienic practices. If one is not careful, his or her poor hygiene while using a catheter could cause infections.

Waking up at two in the morning to urinate was very stressful. I would be so angry that I had to do a whole entire process just to use the bathroom. I would be half asleep, and all I would want was go to the bathroom and go back to bed, but I couldn't. If the bladder doesn't get completely emptied, urine travels back into the kidneys, and that can lead to real health issues. Being in a wheelchair puts you in an uncomfortable space. Constantly needing someone's assistance, feeling as if you are being a bother or an inconvenience, or even breaking down the wheelchair or putting it together when getting in or out of the car can be really taxing on a person. Sometimes, I would be running late and would realize I left my car keys in the house after I spent time breaking down my wheelchair and putting it in the car. It would be so frustrating that I would want to scream and yell.

At times, I would just sit in the car and feel sorry for myself. I would think: *You have two choices. You can stay in the car and feel sorry for yourself, or you can stop letting your emotions throw you off track.* I would wipe my face off, breathe, calm myself down, and once I would get it together, I would put the wheelchair together, get in the chair, go get the keys, and repeat the process when I got back. The only way you grow is by getting stretched and to get stretched, you must get uncomfortable.

1. How comfortable are you with being uncomfortable?

2. What are three things that make you uncomfortable but are major factors in your success?

3. When are you ready to start getting uncomfortable to reach a high level of success?

Deciding to go back to school and chase my education instead of the streets was very uncomfortable for me because I was raised with no love for education. At times, it felt like torture. What prepared me for the school decision was being in a wheelchair. You see, I had been in a wheelchair for a couple of years already, and it allowed me to look at the school process from a different perspective. When I first got confined to the wheelchair, I was terrified of what was ahead. However, once I got comfortable with being uncomfortable, my life started to shape itself the right way.

For about twelve years, I had three jobs. I worked at Seven Hills, a nursing home, where I advocated and cared for the mentally and physically disabled on top of working as an instructor in my barber school, Rob Roy Academy. One day I decided I wanted to open a barbershop. I had never taken a business class, and I didn't go to college to be an entrepreneur, so I was almost scared because I had no knowledge in the world of business ownership. However, after deciding to put everything I had into opening the shop anyway, I realized that I was putting myself in the most uncomfortable position I had ever been in since becoming paraplegic. I realized along the way that a lot of people, including me at that point, had no problem going after the dream. It was the process to get the dream that I didn't want to go through. I learned it wasn't all light work after becoming a CEO. I had just gone part-time at my other two jobs and full time at my shop. I was so uncomfortable with spreading myself so thin, and after some time, I was so tired all the time that I stopped going out with my friends. I went to work, and I came home to my family, and at times, it became depressing, but I continued to be tired and uncomfortable. I knew at the end of all the hard work, I would have my dreams. I would have what I was working for. After some time, my business became successful and started booming. I stepped up from just barbering to cosmetology, and I found myself on the Massachusetts Board of Cosmetology all because I got comfortable being uncomfortable and never gave up. I was able to quit my jobs and run my businesses and not just work in them. I encourage you to create your dream and get specific with the details of it and get to work! Don't give up or get tired because it gets uncomfortable because then you would have brought yourself that far for nothing! Put in that work no matter how long it takes you will get you where you want to be.

CHAPTER 9

❖

Your Reason to Want More

At the age of 15, my only reason for wanting more was just to have money, cars, women, respect, and power. It didn't matter what I had to do to get want I wanted, I was going to do it. It was all I saw as a child, so that's what I learned. By the age of six, I was being exposed to fighting, alcohol, drugs, and verbal abuse in my own household on a regular basis. For years, I saw my grandfather and uncle smoking, drinking, fighting, stealing and shooting up heroine. This was a catalyst for me to start doing and selling drugs, carrying and using guns, and immersing myself in gang activities. We, as humans, tend to mimic the behaviors of others, and this is why some people say, "You are who you walk with." Wanting to be what I saw around me, led to my life as a paraplegic by the age of seventeen. Realizing that someone else's reality did not have to be my reality was a game changer. Looking back now as a husband, father, CEO of my own companies, and author, I am grateful I finally broke the negative family cycle. The reason to want more comes from the hunger of success.

Having a child changed my life. When you have a 9-pound, 14-inch baby angel in your arms, you feel terrified and jubilant at the same time. She changed my life instantly and forever. She had beautiful brown eyes, chunky legs and arms, and tons of hair. It was love at first sight. Her mother and I gave temporary custody to my mother because we could not realistically take care of our daughter while still being involved in the streets. We wanted more for her than what we could provide at the time, and more than anything, we wanted her to be safe.

Have you ever found yourself feeling trapped in life? Do you know what needs to be done to get out? When you do not handle your business, the consequences will hurt you and will not allow you to make proper shifts. Here are some examples of making the proper shift:

1. Aspire to be great.
2. When feeling trapped in life and everything seems like it is hitting you from every angle, stop, reset, and adjust.
3. Find someone who will bring value into your space by coaching you through the proper process and give you step-by-step instructions.

CHAPTER 10

❖

Consistency In Your Routine

Since the age of six, I can recall inconsistency in my family. There was not any structure or routine in our daily lives. Coming from a long line of generational welfare recipients and uneducated individuals, the only consistency I was ever experienced was not to celebrate education, not graduate high school, not have a career or work, and always be confrontational in any situations. The first time I was exposed to the power of routine consistency was on the football field in my freshman year of high school. On the football field, our coach demanded constant consistency in everything we did. He also required consistency in the classroom and outside of school. He always told us how important it was to carry ourselves with the highest level of character including our performance on the field, grades, attitude, and overall leadership. To achieve the highest level of success in any aspect of your life, you must be consistent. For me to do what I wanted, which was playing football, I needed to create the right habits. You see, the coach did not care whether or not I was accustomed to having the right habits to perform at his standards. Players either handled their business, or they did not play.

In your life right now, are you producing or not? Everyone wants to be celebrated without paying a price. Celebration only comes after consistency in your daily routine to be better. Are you executing and producing, or are you waiting for someone to walk up to you and say, "Hey, I believe you're an amazing person. So here, I am giving you all the success you need." For me to be on the team and have a starting position, I needed to be consistent by showing up to practice, exercising, and learning all the coach's plays. The objectives were to compete at a high-level and win games. I quickly realized why the coach always had us running up and down the field practicing the same plays over and over prior to each game. The only way to win games was to minimize our mistakes, and the only way to achieve that was by practicing constantly.

The minute that I realized I was going to be a paraplegic for the rest of my life, I knew I had to use some of the methods that my coach taught us on the field so I could win in the game of life. I realized that in order to have a great quality of life, I needed to be consistent with whom I choose to surround myself. I needed to change my behavior so I could get different results in my life. The coach would have us constantly run the same plays day in and day out. We would go over the same play multiple times per week for hours at a time. The coach knew for us to create a winning mindset we needed to create the right habits. The way to create the right habits is to constantly work on the behaviors. Due to the coach programming us with the right habits and winning mindset, we had a perfect winning streak.

With only two games left in the season, we thought no one could beat us. The consistency in practicing had us looking like a moving, breathing Division I college machine. We started to relax and feel as if we did not have to continue to practice with the same intensity or regularity as we had been doing all year long. Our mindset was that we only had two games left, and they would be automatic wins. Throughout the whole week, the coach would remind us that consistency would allow us to achieve the perfect season with a perfect record, but we were so convinced that we practiced so much during the season that we did not have to practice anymore.

Our lack of preparation was evident when we played the second to the last game. We were not ready to compete. We got pounded, tackled, and hurt. Our plays were not executed the way they should have been. Players on our team were dropping balls, missing certain blocks, and running the wrong routes. Ultimately, we paid the price for not being consistent in our practice, workouts, and playbook preparation, and we lost the game. That perfect season came to an end really quickly. We were so disappointed in ourselves, and at that moment, I *truly* realized the power of being consistent in everything you do in life if you want to achieve the highest level. The power of doing something over and over gives you the confidence and ability to achieve greatness.

We went back the following week and won the final game of the season, but that one loss reminded everyone on our team that in life you have to be consistent in everything you do to achieve greatness. This consistency includes studying and relationships. You cannot get accustomed to turning your effort and preparation on and off whenever you decide. It definitely will have some bad repercussions in your life. A lack of consistency will affect everything you touch and do in life.

On the first day of barbering school, I remember my instructor looking at me and telling me how important consistency is in professional barbering. She reminded me that for me to achieve the levels of a master barber I needed to create the habit of consistency. I would have to be consistent in how I carry myself as a professional, how I communicate with clients, and how I cut hair. She always reminded me that consistency will get me to the level of mastery. I had many challenges as I worked my way through barbering school. I was a paraplegic, I had trouble communicating with people, and I didn't know how to cut hair. However, I knew I had to continue to work on myself and remain consistent day in and day out. I had to continue to show up each day despite my challenges.

Being consistent in your attendance is the first key to success. By showing up daily, you will get comfortable and build up your confidence. Every time I picked up a pair of clippers, I would get terrified, sick to my stomach even. I didn't know how to start or finish the haircuts, but I started with just turning on the machines and asking what type of haircut they wanted. I understood that being consistent with just picking up the clippers would help me get better. One of the reasons we do not succeed is we fail to remain consistent with our daily routines which can get us to the next level. You do not have to be the best, the smartest, the strongest, or have superior qualifications. If you just show up and allow yourself to think, "*No matter what is against me and no matter what it takes, I am going to continue to show up and give it my all.*" If you believe these principles and believe you can be successful, eventually you'll start to gain confidence. When you are confident, you will start seeing the small wins. I know that if you give it everything you have, the only way is up. The goal is to grow and be better than yesterday. As long as you are better than yesterday, you are winning today. As I said before, the main ingredient to your success is consistency.

As a paraplegic, I have many challenges and many things going against me, but I understood at an early age that for me to become a successful barber, I needed to achieve certain things. The number one thing I needed to do was become consistent and show up. I remember the first barbershop in which

I worked straight out of barber school. When I first arrived for the interview, the manager appeared to be thinking, *How are you going to be able to cut hair from you wheelchair?* Truthfully, I had the same thoughts. I had just completed the thousand hours required from the State of Massachusetts, but I did not have any confidence in my ability to perform as a professional barber. Even though I was scared and did not have the confidence, I knew the power of showing up and being consistent would eventually help me become better. I assured the manager that I was his guy even though I just finished barber school. The one thing I knew I could deliver was showing up daily and being reliable. He looked at me, and I could tell he was not sure if he should take the chance to allow me to be one of his barbers. After a few seconds, he said, "Let's give it a try."

I remember being introduced to the rest of the barbers on the first day. All the barbers in the barbershop had been cutting hair over 6 to 10 years. All I had was one year of schooling and no barbershop experience. Imagine how scary the situation was for me. In my heart, I understood the power of showing up and being consistent in everything I did. It is all I had as a paraplegic especially in an industry that consists of barbers standing behind the barber chair for 8 to 12 hours daily. I had to learn how to cut hair sitting down. Being in school and cutting hair with instructions to help you is one thing, but working in the barbershop and not having someone to guide you or walk you through any situation you experience was another ball game. As scared as I was, I had a choice at the time to either go through the process or just quit.

Many times, I doubted myself, but one thing I knew about myself was that I understood the power of consistency. I learned it on the football field when we almost had a perfect season, but we did not remain consistent; that always stuck with me. I came into the barber industry with the same mentality. As long as I could show up daily and give it everything I had, I knew everything would be great. With hard work, consistency, and willingness to get uncomfortable, I eventually would get to a point where I would be able to say, "I am a master barber."

I remember starting that week and having clients look at me as if they were wondering how I would be able to cut hair sitting down. The majority of the clients already had their own barbers, and the rest of the walk-ins did not want to sit down in my chair. None of the clients wanted to take a chance on the new barber especially one who could not stand. I didn't cut anyone for several weeks and that eventually turned into a couple months. I started doubting myself all over again. I would question myself multiple times per day and wonder, *"Is this really for me?"* I thought, *"I don't think I can do it!"* I was licensed. I finished school with my diploma in barbering, but it didn't mean anything if I did not put in the work at the shop. I promise you I was so discouraged and embarrassed that I didn't even want to show up for work. When I felt defeated, I reminded myself of the importance of staying confident and showing up.

Eventually, I started to see the gaps in the routines of the barbers with whom I worked. They had amazing skills and were very confident in their abilities to execute any service. However, they were not consistent with their professionalism; they were showing up late or not at all. So, I started to say to myself, *"OK, all I have to do is be the first one in the barbershop and the last one out of the barbershop."* Eventually, I would notice some clients waiting for their barbers for hours at a time. I would just sit there and observe the barbers' inconsistencies all day. Since I was often the first barber in the shop and the last person to leave, I started building relationships with all the clients. I consistently would say, "Hi!" to everyone and shake their hands no matter who it was. It could have been someone who was not there to get a haircut or a young child, but I would still introduce myself. I would make sure people knew who I was and that my intention was to cut hair. Clients started to get comfortable with me, and that opened up dialogue, which led to developing relationships. They still were not sitting in my chair for haircuts, but while waiting, they would interact with me. They would ask why I became a barber and what encouraged me to be a barber in a wheelchair. After a while, certain clients would say to me, "You know what? I cannot wait for my barber any longer. I have been waiting here for two hours, and I have to go to work. Do you think you can clean the back of my neck?" Eventually, they would sit in my chair and get some type of service. Once some clients took a chance on me by sitting in my chair, the other clients watched me cut. My confidence was building up by having clients in my chair. As time went on, I felt the impact of the consistency of coming to the barbershop and saying *"Hi!"* to everyone whether they were young kids, mothers, fathers, other barbers, or anyone who was willing to engage in dialogue with me. Staying consistent with the same routine was my recipe for success. I was not the one with the best skills or longest time in the industry. I did not have the nicest clothes, and I was not the tallest person. However, no one in that barbershop could out work my consistency.

Overall, clients just wanted to get a haircut and enjoy themselves while engaging in some great conversation with their barber. They didn't want to spend hours at the shop because of an unreliable barber. Not giving up on myself when everything seemed impossible and when everyone doubted and laughed at me allowed me to position myself in the beauty industry as a guru. I went out and opened multiple barbershops and salons across the city. I made a name for myself not because I was the best barber but because I provided the best professional service on a constant basis.

As a paraplegic, I have to be able to compete in all aspects of my life. As you read this story on how I had to overcome many challenges in my daily personal and business routine, consider the areas of your life you can improve by just showing up and being consistent with what you do. I wanted to aspire to be better in my life, and I always have challenged myself to be a better version of me. I need you to know the fear of not being able to succeed will kick in, but I am here to tell you that fear is not real. Even though you feel you are not enough because you do not have the proper G.P.A., friends, relationships, parents, classmates, etc., you have to believe in yourself before anyone believes in you. You just need to put in the work and be consistent in the process. Aspire to want more, create a plan, stay consistent with the process, and then execute your goals. It is that simple. If I can come from a broken home, be a ninth grade dropout, be gunned down at the age of 17 in front of my mother, and come back and dominate an industry, you have everything you need to achieve success in your life.

After 20 years, I have achieved the highest levels in the barber and beauty industry. I am a master barber, Class 1 cosmetologist, barber/cosmetology instructor, state evaluator, and I am part of the cosmetology and barbering board in the State of Massachusetts. Not only do I educate students and test at a state level, but also I reprimand any barber engaging in unlawful business practices in the State of Massachusetts. I share this to encourage you not to be scared and to get started on your journey to greatness. I do not have any artistic skills, but I was determined to learn the skills to communicate, run a business, be a platform artist, travel across the country with

FROM PARALYZED TO PROSPEROUS

with powerful and influential people, be involved in creating barber battles with celebrity barbers, and cut and compete on a national barbering platform. The only reason I was able to achieve everything was by being consistent with who I am and focusing on what I was able to bring to the table. I was not the best at my profession, but I wanted to excel more than others barbers. I need you to start now and avoid letting your situation define who you are. Go be amazing!!!

Consider the following questions as you strive to *Level Up*:

1. What are the 3 things you need to start doing on a consistent basis?

2. What are the 3 things you need to stop doing?

CHAPTER 11

❖

Living Your Best Life

As I sit here and think back on my early years in school, I remember struggling with who I was as a person. Some people would say that is too early in a child's life to determine his or her passion, gift, or purpose in life. I remember not being comfortable with anything. I would go to art class and really give it everything I had, but it never came out as the teacher instructed or as any other kid's art in the classroom. I always would be insecure with singing, dancing, drawing, and playing instruments and sports. I went through elementary school comparing myself to everyone, especially those with their natural gifts at an early age. I can remember having classmates who had amazing grades in either drawing, singing, dancing, or sports.

Once I started middle school, things didn't get any easier for me. The pressure doubled. I was concerned with girls, homework, classwork, and sports. If you could name it, I was concerned about it. I worried that I was ugly and too fat. I thought that I didn't dress well enough or speak English well enough, and the list went on. The boys always tried to compete in everything. It was always a challenge to fit in at school. There was so much going on that I was totally lost regarding who I *really* was and what my gift and purpose was in life.

I remember when I started to be disrespectful and destructive in class just to fit in. In seventh grade, I had a teacher by the name of Mr. Goldberg. Mr. Goldberg had a huge fish tank filled with several different species of fish, and one of the students dared me to pour some iodine in the tank. To this day, I remember Mr. Goldberg's face and reaction when he found out what I did. I got suspended, my grandmother had to pay for the fish, and I also received the whooping of my life. I felt terrible about it and still do to this day, and what hurt me the most was the fact that I willingly hurt someone just to get a laugh.

From that incident, I learned never to entertain myself at someone else's expense. I had to start asking myself if I wanted to be a problem or a solution. I started to be intentional in terms of how I acted. I was no longer going to be a follower. If I was going to get in trouble, it would not be because someone else encouraged me to do it, it would be *my* decision. Too many times, we let someone else dictate how we carry ourselves. Stop letting individuals talk you into being disrespectful, disruptive, and dishonest just because you are still trying to find yourself. Being stuck in this place affects your happiness, your health, and your relationships and it can be very painful to go through and deal with.

While you find yourself, you have to love yourself while doing so. Going through middle school and high school is very challenging and scary. So, instead of waiting for others to love you, love yourself first. The only true love is self-love, and when you have self-love you are not worried about anyone's opinion of you. You know that even though you are not perfect, you are an amazing human being, and you have everything it takes to become amazing in life. Take it from me, I have been losing since I can remember, and that did not change until I started having self-love. Look in the mirror and remind yourself that you are the king or queen of your own space.

As I entered my freshman year of high school, I still did not have a clear view of my gift or purpose in life, but I started to realize the gift of my presence. I did not talk to many students or teachers at the school, but I would occasionally be at the right place at the right time. At times, I would have to step in to diffuse certain situations such as someone being disrespected or bullied. Once I disrespected Mr. Goldberg, I shifted my mindset and no longer wanted to be a part of anyone being hurt. If you are watching someone in school being bullied in any way, and you choose not to intervene, you are just as much to blame. Please do not forget your presence is a gift. Step in and make a difference in someone's life as often as you can.

Do you know your purpose? Everyone has a purpose in life and within that purpose lies a unique talent just waiting to be expressed and shared with the world. I found my purpose through playing high school football. It was not my ability to play the game, but it was my ability to become a leader and lead with good intentions. At the time, I did not realize what purpose meant, but as I think back, I always had the gift. As you enter high school and try to find your identity, please do not compromise your character as I did in Mr. Goldberg's class. Look around yourself and see how you can use your gift for good. If you are going through any bad experiences at home or in school, please reach out to someone who can help you. Too many times, we let situations get the best of us when we do not have to go through them on our own. Remember, self-love is a major key to success in life and in finding your purpose and what feeds your passion. What do you love doing? It is usually something you can do without effort and actually enjoy doing. Your circle of influence has to be individuals who create value in your journey of life. Whether at home or in school, you have a choice about who you decide to allow into your circle of trust. Get around givers and not takers. By doing that, you will eliminate any insecurities and worries. Start living your best life. You should not be ashamed of who you are. Be patient with yourself and do not compare yourself to anyone. You are unique in your own way so surround yourself with people who celebrate you instead of just tolerate you. There is no need to look around for approval when you know what is right, and you know what your heart wants. I give you permission to be yourself and truly live in your purpose. I had to take my weaknesses and turn them into strengths to show the world nothing is impossible in life. Life is what you make it! Go out and be amazing.

CHAPTER 12

❖

Kicking Your Wheelchair

In my early teens, I made a lot of bad decisions, and some I'm still paying for at the age of 43. In life, there are always effects of the decisions that we make. At the age of 15, I decided to drop out of school and join a street gang. I involved myself with drugs, guns, and any other street activity you can imagine. I went from the football field to the war zone, and I justified my actions with poor excuses. The honest truth was that I chose to do what was easier at the time. Dropping out was easier than bringing up my grades and staying in school to earn my high school diploma. I blamed my family, teachers, students, the school, and everyone else for my situation in life. The truth was, I was the only one to blame. Dropping out of school gave me all the time in the world to screw up my own life. With no place to go, I had plenty of time to hang out without realizing I was destroying my life with every decision I made. By the age of 17, I immersed myself completely in the street life becoming a full-blown gang member in a wheelchair with a newborn baby girl.

Having my daughter changed my mindset. Even though I knew I needed to change my lifestyle, it was easier said than done. Once I made the decisions, I had to apply action steps. The growing pains hurt, but I had to start thinking as a father and not as a paraplegic dropout and gang member. If you are going through anything in life such as an addiction, gangs, depression, or abuse, you can and will overcome it just like I did. The first step is wanting to change, the second step is staying out of your emotions. The reason you are not winning is not because someone is hating on you. You are stuck in your emotions and hanging onto the pain someone else caused you. You are going through life blaming everyone else for the reason your life is upside down. When you stay in your emotions, it's an automatic loss on your behalf. Once you control your emotions, dominate your space. In a few chapters in this book, I spoke about how I took my weaknesses and turned them into my strengths. That's how I was able to dominate everything around me.

Find individuals who can provide you with the blueprint. It can be someone in your family, school, or organization who can coach, mentor, or guide you to the right path. There are no limits to how amazing you can live your life. I came into the beauty industry and dominated it for over 20 years as a paraplegic. You can achieve anything you put your mind to do. The only limitations you will experience will be the ones you place on yourself. I truly believe that life is what you make of it. I chose to dropout. I chose to have a kid. I chose to gang bang. I almost lost my life and my mother's life as well. The moment I decided to receive a better quality of life, I dominated the barber industry and went back to get my G.E.D. And after all my hard work and dedication, I received a proclamation which makes January 6th *Jorge A. Sierra Day* in Worcester, Massachusetts.

Even after being so successful in my career, I still had a mental handicap. I was still dealing with insecurities of being confined to a wheelchair. At the time, I dealt with feeling less than a real man, and those feelings turned into depression. I felt that no woman would look at me as a real man. I felt people would not have any respect for a person sitting in a wheelchair. I didn't like how I looked because from my waist down. Everything was extremely skinny. I would be extremely embarrassed that I would have to use catheters to empty my bladder every time I had to use the bathroom. At times, I would have accidents on myself due to not being able to control my bowel movements, and eventually I started to wear diapers to prevent certain accidents in front of people. Even though I was very successful and always had a smile on my face, I was really devastated inside. I was still dealing with a mental wheelchair. I had to stop fooling myself if I truly wanted to be free in life. I could not continue to go around and ask people to lose their mental wheelchairs, and I still had one. I had conquered everything in business, but I still needed to conquer myself as an individual by being the best father, the best husband, and the best leader overall.

The last time I had a skin break down, it turned into a serious ulcer and a bone infection and I wound up being hospitalized for a year. My bed in the nursing home became the place where I got baths and where I urinated and had bowel movements. Going through that, I almost lost everything including my job as an educator, my business that I had for over 16 years, and most importantly, my fiancé. I did not want to live my life with doubt, fear, worries, depression, confusion, and a lack of self-love.

When I was discharged from the nursing home, my mindset shifted. I truly was ready to kick my mental wheelchair. First, I decided that enough was enough. Once I made the decision, I started working on my comeback. I was around 300 pounds and looked like a caveman. I knew the first thing I needed to do was start losing weight. For several months, I ate 6 times a day, every 3 hours. It was torture, but once I started seeing results I got the confidence and the energy to go harder.

Today, I don't care that I have skinny legs and an uneven body. I kept myself from standing over the last 20 years because I was concerned about people's opinions of me, but once I started standing, I started to take steps too. As scary as it was, I was on cloud nine with all the progress I was achieving. There is nothing better than the love I had for myself. I started to go to the gym, continued to eat my meals and eventually everyone could see the transformation. Once the compliments and encouragements started to come, I locked in and went into beast mode. Today, I am walking over 200 feet at a time with a walker. I also do 45 minutes of cardio on a gym bicycle six times a week, and I can go up and down three flights of stairs. I finally took the steps to remove my mental barriers when I stopped worrying about how I looked, what people's opinions were of me, and whether or not I had what it took to become who I wanted to be.

For the last 20 years, I have had the opportunity to open and operate multiple businesses and travel across the country and soon, the world. Your perspective in life is everything. Change your outlook. Most people say their cup is half-empty or half-full, but in reality, when you look at it, it's a blessing to even have a cup to fill. When you have the cup, you can always fill it or empty it if you choose. Having the cup means you're the cup. Every day you open your eyes and have another day of life is a huge game changer.

I challenge you to identify your mental wheelchair and figure out why it is it that you are not able to get to the next level. What is keeping you from growing in your business and your relationships? Once you are tired of losing, I challenge you to come up with a plan; once you come up with a plan, I want you to execute that plan. The only way to get over a mental wheelchair is to identify your problem and get started on your plan even if you feel it is not a perfect plan.

Start Now! Begin working on yourself. Remember, self-love is everything! No one can take the pain that you have inside away but you. No one can make you do anything you do not want to do. However, if you are like me, and you are tired of being tired and tired of feeling discouraged, depressed and uncertain, I encourage you to just get started NOW. If I can start walking after 24 years of being a paraplegic, you also can WALK into greatness. Please identify what is holding you back and kick the mental wheelchair away. Go be amazing and WALK in your purpose!